C000183628

# Manifest
## YOUR
## WAY TO
# Happiness

LYDIA LEVINE

summersdale

MANIFEST YOUR WAY TO HAPPINESS

Text by Holly Brook-Piper

An Hachette UK Company
www.hachette.co.uk

Summersdale Publishers Ltd
Part of Octopus Publishing Group Limited
Carmelite House
50 Victoria Embankment
LONDON
EC4Y 0DZ
UK

www.summersdale.com

Printed and bound in Poland

ISBN: 978-1-80007-917-5

Substantial discounts on bulk quantities of Summersdale books are available to corporations, professional associations and other organizations. For details contact general enquiries: telephone: +44 (0) 1243 771107 or email: enquiries@summersdale.com.

To:....................................

From:................................

## ARE YOU READY TO MAKE YOUR DREAMS A REALITY?

The universe is ready and waiting to help you manifest your way to happiness so you can live your best life!

Manifestation is one of the most powerful tools we have at our disposal, and the good news is, anyone can try it! But what is it? It's the practice of believing and affirming positive thoughts with the aim of making them real by proactively taking action to get what you want, with help from the universe.

It follows the fundamental principles of the law of attraction, where positive thoughts can produce positive results in your life. These thoughts are a form of energy, which the universe responds to. By harnessing your positive energy, you can attract happiness in all areas of your life. It's important to remember, what you put out is what you will receive back, so beware: if you have negative thoughts, the law of attraction says that you will attract negative experiences in your life.

Everyone's definition of happiness looks different depending on their circumstances; for some, happiness is intrinsically linked to love or friendship, while others feel that their happiness is centred on abundance or success. This book will help you to identify and clarify your goals for reaching ultimate happiness, providing you with everything you need to start manifesting the life of your dreams.

The world of manifesting can seem confusing with so many terms and techniques, but try not to feel overwhelmed. It will work in different ways for everyone; there isn't necessarily a "right" way to go about it.

You have the power to make your dreams a reality, so start manifesting now to find your happy.

Embrace the law of attraction.
If you focus on the positives in life,
positivity will be attracted to you.
Likewise, with negative thinking,
if you put out negative energy, you
will attract negative experiences.

The universe is made up of energy that is constantly "vibrating". Since like attracts like, these vibrations will attract others of a similar frequency. This applies to your thoughts as well. Positive thoughts have a higher frequency, whereas negative ones are lower. By focusing on positive thoughts, you can raise your vibrating frequency.

**Ask for what
you want and
be prepared
to get it.**

MAYA ANGELOU

Once you are open to the universe being able to give you what you want, it is time to let it know your ultimate dreams and desires. One way of doing this is through visualization. Use this technique to provide you with focus and motivation, while helping you to identify what it is you want to manifest.

While manifestation is based upon the power of your positive thoughts, there are several items that you could invest in to aid your manifesting.

## MANIFESTING TOOL #1

A notebook and pen are vital for the scripting technique (see page 44). Choose one that is special to you.

## MANIFESTING TOOL #2

A selection of crystals can supercharge your energy. Different crystals have different vibrations that can be used to enhance your own energy. Common ways of utilizing the power of crystals are wearing them as jewellery, holding them during manifesting and placing them in various spots around the home that are linked to your goals.

*Go confidently in the direction of your dreams. Live the life you have imagined.*

HENRY DAVID THOREAU

## MANIFESTING TOOL #3

Candles can be used during manifesting to create an ambient, uplifting space. Candles have been used as spiritual tools for centuries in many religions, with some believing they can cleanse negative feelings and offer clarity. Try lighting a candle, in a safe spot, to create a calm, soothing atmosphere to help raise your vibrations during your manifesting.

## MANIFESTING TOOL #4

Sage, when burned, is said to
clear negative energy in the home.
"Smudging", the act of burning
herbs, may lift your mood, and
therefore your vibrations. If you
do burn anything, make sure you
research how to do it safely, and do
not do it around children or pets.

## MANIFESTING TOOL #5

Music can be an effective tool while manifesting. It has the ability to enhance your feelings – upbeat music can raise your energy whereas ballads can make you melancholy. If you choose to listen to music, make sure it's music that makes you feel good. No breakup songs when manifesting love; no sad songs when manifesting joy!

Be patient and trust the universe. Everything happens for a reason and you will be okay.

ARIANA GRANDE

Do you know what it is that you want to manifest? It might be that you've had the same dream for years and it's completely mapped out in your mind, or it may be that you don't really know what you want from life. If it's the latter, don't panic, this book will help you work it out!

Visualization is one of the most popular manifestation methods. It is all about using the power of the mind to make your desires feel real. Once you have identified your ultimate goals, keep reiterating them in your mind to reprogramme your brain to believe you can and will succeed. Eventually your subconscious will start to come up with ways to achieve them.

How to use visualization:

✦ Sit comfortably with your eyes closed and imagine, in as much detail as possible, what your life will look like when your manifestations are achieved. Make sure you are viewing the scene from your own perspective and be aware of all your senses. Set aside a few minutes every day to complete this exercise.

Whether you
think you can or
can't – either way,
you are right.

**HENRY FORD**

To make your visualization as clear as possible, answer the following questions:

+ What can you see?

+ What can you hear?

+ What can you feel?

+ How do you appear?

+ Who else is in your visualization?

+ What emotions are you feeling?

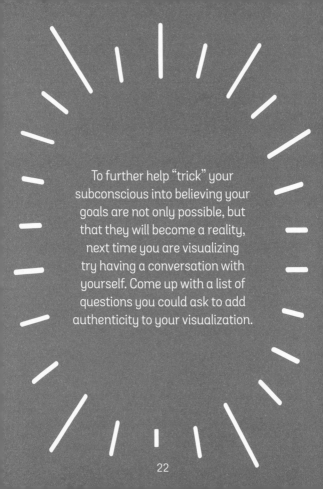

To further help "trick" your subconscious into believing your goals are not only possible, but that they will become a reality, next time you are visualizing try having a conversation with yourself. Come up with a list of questions you could ask to add authenticity to your visualization.

I am
creating the
life of
my dreams

There are no rules as to when you should visualize, however you might find that doing it before bed works well as there should be fewer chances of being distracted. Try to commit to spending at least 15 minutes a day visualizing. If you do it regularly it should become a habit.

It's our intention. Our intention is everything. Nothing happens on this planet without it. Not one single thing has ever been accomplished without intention.

JIM CARREY

Visualization isn't a "one size fits all". Once you've given it a go a few times, you can start to tailor it to what you feel works best. It may be that you find listening to music distracting, but meditation works well (see pages 62–63). Everyone's journey looks different.

I can achieve anything I put my mind to

A vision board is a fantastic manifesting tool. In essence, it is a visual representation of your manifestation. It should be filled with items that embody the dreams and desires you are manifesting. This is a great way to help clarify your goals and provide motivation. Have it somewhere you will see it every day.

What you will need to create a vision board:

✦  A large piece of card

✦  Scissors

✦  Glue or sticky tape

✦  Pens and/or paint

✦  Photos, postcards, inspiring quotes,
   cuttings from magazines, drawings
   – anything that can be stuck down
   to represent your dreams

✦  Imagination!

*Once you make a decision, the universe conspires to make it happen.*

RALPH WALDO EMERSON

You've had fun completing your vision board, so now what? It's time to believe! Sitting in front of your board, concentrate your mind on the future you will have. For 10–15 minutes a day, imagine what you will be doing in your new, happy life, and how it feels.

Why not take a photo of your vision board so you can refer to it throughout the day?

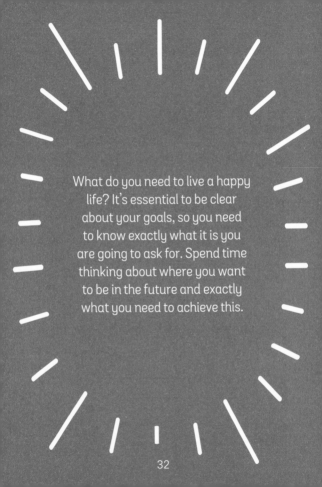

What do you need to live a happy life? It's essential to be clear about your goals, so you need to know exactly what it is you are going to ask for. Spend time thinking about where you want to be in the future and exactly what you need to achieve this.

While it's important to focus hard on manifesting what you want, there is work involved as well. You can't just sit back and wait for good things to happen; you need to be proactive at making your dreams a reality too. For example, if you're manifesting to become a popular influencer, you must be on social media!

You get in
life what you
have the courage
to ask for.

OPRAH WINFREY

Use manifestation as a tool for achieving your best life, but don't expect it to solve all your problems overnight. Manifestation isn't magic; it takes time, effort and perseverance. If you are willing to embrace this, the world is your oyster. Open your mind to good things and good things will happen!

My life is open to
abundance while
I am grateful for
everything I have

Instagram, TikTok and Pinterest are good places to check out tips and inspiration for manifesting. Social media is a great way to share your positive energy with like-minded people, who are all on the path to their best lives. Why not contribute some of the things you have found interesting and useful?

An affirmation is a positive statement to help you overcome negative thoughts. Using the affirmations included in this book for inspiration, write some of your own. By repeating these daily, you can challenge and alter negative thoughts you may be holding on to and reaffirm your belief that you can and will succeed. Always use present tense, e.g. "I am", "I have", "I feel", and be specific.

Keep your mind fixed
on what you want in life:
not on what you don't want.

NAPOLEON HILL

Best crystals for manifesting:

**Happiness and joy:** Celestite, citrine, black tourmaline

**Money and success:** Pyrite, tiger's eye, green aventurine

**Love:** Rose quartz, moonstone, pink kunzite, rhodonite

**Health:** Obsidian, garnet, quartz, amethyst

**Creativity:** Carnelian, hematite, lapis lazuli

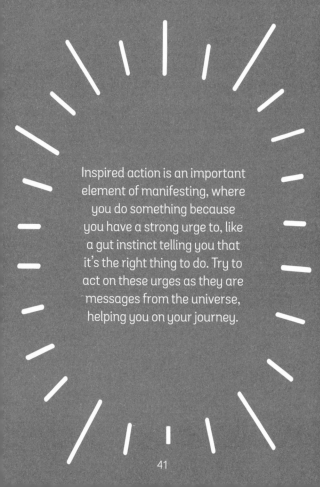

Inspired action is an important element of manifesting, where you do something because you have a strong urge to, like a gut instinct telling you that it's the right thing to do. Try to act on these urges as they are messages from the universe, helping you on your journey.

"Manifestation blocks" are obstacles that come up that work against you manifesting your dreams. These could be any number of things – not trusting the process, doubting yourself, or the inability to break bad habits. The first way to overcome manifestation blocks is to identify them and try to solve them.

Always go with
your passions.
Never ask
yourself if it's
realistic or not.

DEEPAK CHOPRA

A popular manifesting tool is the scripting technique, where you write down the life you want to manifest, enabling you to explore your desires in detail on paper. This is great if you struggle with visualization. Always keep your scripting so you can see how far you've come!

Don't get overwhelmed and tone down your dreams because you don't want to ask for too much. Try to block out other people's negative attitudes and expectations of what they think you are capable of. Anything is possible; you just have to manifest it!

Everything I do brings me success and happiness

Always consider others when mapping out your manifestations. Whatever you decide upon, make sure it doesn't have the potential to harm others. Think carefully about your responsibilities – you don't want to regret your decision. If the universe thinks you're doing things for the wrong reasons, it won't respond.

*If you have a positive frame of mind, you can manifest positive things in your life.*

ALESHA DIXON

One of the most important things to remember when manifesting your dreams is to stay positive. Don't forget that the central tenet of manifesting is that positivity attracts positivity. Good thoughts only! If you are struggling, look back at your goals for motivation and inspiration. Good things are coming your way if you believe in them!

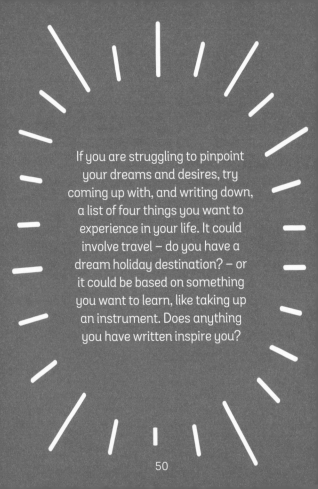

If you are struggling to pinpoint your dreams and desires, try coming up with, and writing down, a list of four things you want to experience in your life. It could involve travel – do you have a dream holiday destination? – or it could be based on something you want to learn, like taking up an instrument. Does anything you have written inspire you?

Try not to let financial limitations rule your manifestations. When determining what you want to ask the universe for, approach it from a place where money is no object.

Acknowledging
the good that you
already have in your
life is the foundation
for all abundance.

ECKHART TOLLE

Just because you've had the same dream for years, it doesn't mean that it's still the right one for you. Don't rush into manifesting what you think you want – sit down and really evaluate it first. Make sure it's something that you still desire and which will benefit you and your life.

# I trust
# my journey

Keep believing in yourself and have faith in the universe delivering. If you don't believe, your dreams will never become a reality. Don't let your doubts become manifestation blocks (see page 42). Banish those self-defeating thoughts and dream big.

You aren't limited to asking for physical things. Some people will ask the universe for a new job, whereas others will ask for the confidence to apply for new employment. If you're feeling anxious or stressed, you could manifest the ability to feel calm and relaxed. The sky is the limit!

If you can dream it,
you can do it.

WALT DISNEY

If you are making big changes to your life, try breaking down your manifestations into smaller goals. Be proactive and look at the bigger picture; this way you will be able to have a clearer focus on the steps you need to take to attain the ultimate dream of happiness.

Have a little patience!
Give yourself and the universe
time to deliver and make sure
you are always on the lookout
for ways to make your goals a
reality sooner. What comes your
way might not look exactly as
you envisaged, but it could be a
stepping stone, so don't dismiss
opportunities as they arise.

You can change your mind.
Yes, you may have put a lot of
thought and energy into manifesting
one thing but ultimately, if it is no
longer feeling like the right thing for
you, just stop. It takes real courage
to do this. Listen to your heart and
don't feel embarrassed – feel proud!

**Thoughts become things. If you see it in your mind, you will hold it in your hand.**

BOB PROCTOR

One immensely powerful tool to help raise your vibrations is meditation. The act of meditating can help you to relax and bring you into alignment with the universe, helping to match your vibrations to those of your manifestations. Try to find at least 10–15 minutes a day to meditate.

How to meditate:

1   Find somewhere quiet and comfortable, where you won't be distracted.

2   Focus on your breathing – breathe in through your nose, hold for a couple of seconds and then breathe out through your mouth.

3   Clear your mind of unhelpful thoughts.

4   When you're feeling completely relaxed, you can start to visualize.

# If I put
# my mind to it,
# I will achieve it

Don't let one small setback knock your confidence. If you let one negative thing affect your mindset, it will encourage more negativity. Accept it and move on. Trust in the process!

*I visualized myself being a famous actor and earning big money. I could feel and taste success. I just knew it would all happen.*

ARNOLD SCHWARZENEGGER

Don't just focus on what you don't have; place your concentration on what it is that you want. If you are manifesting abundance, don't fixate on not having it, but consider what it will look like and what you will do when you have it.

Dream big! If you can dream it, you can achieve it. Don't let the fear of failure hold you back. If you don't support your manifestations 100 per cent, you're not going to get what you want. It will be worth it in the end!

If you want good things to happen, you need to feel good about yourself. Help make yourself feel more positive by starting a gratitude journal. Use it to list all the things you are grateful for – no matter how big or small. Show the universe you appreciate what you already have before expecting to receive more.

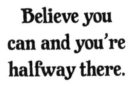

**Believe you
can and you're
halfway there.**

THEODORE ROOSEVELT

If you're struggling to pinpoint exactly what you want for a happy future, ask yourself the following questions for inspiration:

✦ What are your passions?

✦ What would you like to do more of?

✦ What inspires you?

✦ What motivates you?

✦ What are you good at?

✦ Where would you like to be?

I have

limitless

potential

Reframing your mindset to a more positive, open one can be difficult, so don't be hard on yourself if you feel you are slipping back into a negative mindset. If you do, remind yourself of what you are trying to achieve. You've got this!

Try to live every day as if you have already received what you are asking for. Not only should this align your present with your future, but it will also provide motivation for making your dreams become a reality. Have faith!

# Nothing is,
# unless our thinking
# makes it so.

**WILLIAM SHAKESPEARE**

Abundance is a popular manifestation, but it isn't simply about wanting to have lots of money. Financial security is important and not having it can be a great cause of stress and anxiety. To be able to successfully manifest abundance, you need to make sure you believe you are worthy of it, while also appreciating what you have already got.

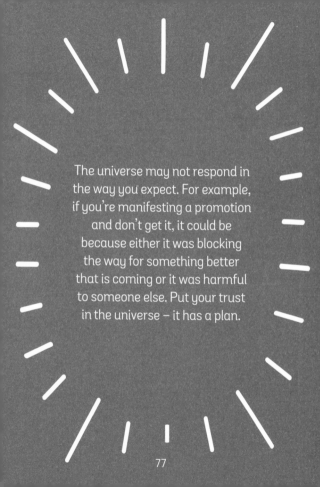

The universe may not respond in the way you expect. For example, if you're manifesting a promotion and don't get it, it could be because either it was blocking the way for something better that is coming or it was harmful to someone else. Put your trust in the universe – it has a plan.

Setting "intentions" is a great way to help you stay motivated. This is where you decide what **you** can do to assist the universe in achieving your manifestations – it's not about **what** you want to achieve but **how** you intend to achieve it. For example, if you are manifesting a new job, you could sign up to a recruitment agency, or if you are manifesting happiness, your intention could be to remain positive.

Reality is created
by the mind.
We can change
our reality by
changing our mind.

PLATO

If love is the key to your happiness, first accept you can only manifest love for yourself; you cannot manifest someone falling in love with you. Let love into your life, and the universe will respond, even if it's not in a way you imagined it would happen.

Write a letter from your future self. It can be one year, five years or even ten years in the future – it's completely up to you! Write it as if you are living the life you are manifesting and include all your achievements. Date the letter and hide it somewhere safe until it's time to retrieve it.

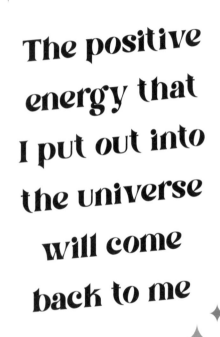

The positive
energy that
I put out into
the universe
will come
back to me

No one said this was easy. Manifesting isn't magic; it's working in collaboration with cosmic forces, so you must act on signs you receive from the universe and take opportunities when they arise to see results. Manifestation isn't going to solve any problems in your life overnight. Have faith, with a little bit of patience and effort thrown in!

*Beware of
what you set
your heart upon.
For it shall
surely be yours.*

RALPH WALDO EMERSON

The focus wheel is a simple yet effective technique to help you visualize and focus on your goals. In the centre circle write down what you want to manifest and around the outside write any positive thoughts relating to it.

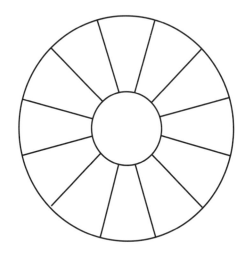

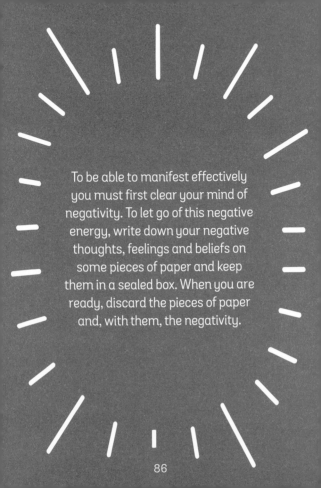

To be able to manifest effectively you must first clear your mind of negativity. To let go of this negative energy, write down your negative thoughts, feelings and beliefs on some pieces of paper and keep them in a sealed box. When you are ready, discard the pieces of paper and, with them, the negativity.

Even if you're not consciously
visualizing and manifesting you
can use spare moments of time
to daydream. This can help you
determine what it is you want
while also feeding information
into your subconscious.

Once you replace
negative thoughts
with positive ones,
you'll start having
positive results.

WILLIE NELSON

Reframe your negative thought patterns to more positive ones. For example, instead of "No one loves me," tell yourself that YOU love yourself and you are open to receiving love from others.

I am ready for
good things to
come my way

Synchronicity is where seemingly unrelated events come together to create meaning. This can include recurring signs that lead you somewhere significant, or being in the right place at the right time to meet someone special. Keep an eye out as these are signs from the universe. You might be seeing these to help you back onto your correct path.

Remember, if you are vibrating at a low frequency, you will attract low energy. Always be aware of the energy you are putting out into the universe as what you put out is what you will receive.

There are no limits to
what you can create for
you because your ability
to think is unlimited!

RHONDA BYRNE

The 55×5 method is based on writing an affirmation 55 times for five days to manifest your chosen intention. By repeatedly writing your affirmation you raise your vibrations, becoming a vibrational match for what you are manifesting. This technique is perfect if you thrive on routine!

How to manifest using
the 55x5 method:

1   Clarify in your mind what it
    is you want to manifest.

2   Consider how achieving
    this manifestation makes
    you feel.

3   Choose an affirmation that
    embodies what you want.

4   Write your affirmation
    down 55 times every day
    for five days. To save you
    time, mark out the 55th
    line so you don't have to
    continuously count where
    you are up to.

If you're feeling worried or stressed, not only will your vibration frequency be low, but you'll also struggle to get in the best mindset for manifesting. Feeling good about yourself is an essential part of manifesting. Practise daily self-care to help foster the right state of mind – try a bubble bath, a walk through nature or watch your favourite TV show to help you relax.

**Fight and push harder for what you believe in, you'd be surprised, you are much stronger than you think.**

LADY GAGA

Believe it or not, one reason why you may not achieve your goals could be down to not having given yourself permission to do so. Utilize the manifesting technique of "permission practice" by telling yourself daily that you deserve to achieve your dreams and desires. Allow yourself to experience what you want out of life – you're the only one who can!

Giving yourself and the universe a set timeline for achieving your manifestations is only going to produce impatience. It's human nature to want total control, but in this case, you just have to trust that the universe has a plan, so keep proactively working towards your goals, while looking out for and responding to the universe's signs. Give it some time!

Every day I
am one step
closer to living
my best life

One great way to show the universe you are thankful and appreciative for everything it provides is by paying the kindness forward. Random acts of kindness are a great way to do this. Not only are you enriching someone else's life, but you are making yourself feel good at the same time and putting more positive energy into the world.

*Everything you can imagine is real.*

PABLO PICASSO

When deciding what you want to manifest, try to examine your "why". This will help you determine if you are manifesting the right things for the right reasons. If you aren't, the universe will know and won't deliver.

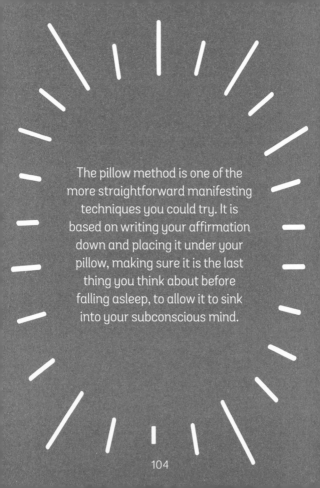

The pillow method is one of the more straightforward manifesting techniques you could try. It is based on writing your affirmation down and placing it under your pillow, making sure it is the last thing you think about before falling asleep, to allow it to sink into your subconscious mind.

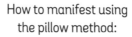

How to manifest using
the pillow method:

1  On a piece of paper, write down an
   affirmation, making sure it is as
   detailed as possible and written in
   the present tense.

2  Place your affirmation under your
   pillow.

3  While falling asleep, concentrate
   your mind on your affirmation.

4  When you wake, remove the
   affirmation from under your
   pillow and keep it somewhere safe
   so you can repeat the process.

Everything you want is out there waiting for you to ask. Everything you want also wants you. But you have to take action to get it.

JACK CANFIELD

Fake it until you make it! The universe may not have responded to your manifestations yet, but that doesn't mean you can't embody the person you plan to become. Align your vibrations with your manifestations to encourage quicker results. Think of it as "Dress for the job you want, not the job you have."

I have
the courage
and the
confidence
to get what
I want

Jim Carrey famously revealed that as part of his journey to manifest success he wrote himself a post-dated cheque for $10 million. Later he was cast in the movie *Dumb and Dumber*. The fee? You guessed it, $10 million! He claimed hard work and visualizing got him there. Can you think of anything you could do like this?

To succeed in manifesting you need to master your subconscious. You do this through "subconscious reprogramming" (or "belief assessment"). This involves identifying pre-existing, negative beliefs that limit you, for example, that you are a failure or that you are unlovable. It's important to explore the origins of these beliefs and debunk them. The more you do this, the more your subconscious will respond and accept new, positive thoughts.

I believe you can speak
things into existence.

JAY-Z

The 3-6-9 manifesting method, based on numerology, centres on the belief that the numbers three, six and nine are spiritually significant and the gateway to the universe. This technique is ideal for beginners as it's simple and can fit into a busy life schedule.

How to use the
3-6-9 technique:

1. Decide what you want. In the morning, as soon as you wake, write it down three times. It must be in the present or past tense.

2. In the afternoon, write down the same affirmation six times.

3. Before you go to bed, write it down nine times.

4. Do this for at least 33 days.

An intention (or manifestation) journal is a dedicated place for you to document what you intend to manifest into reality, how you'll do it, and your thoughts and feelings about your journey. Through regular use you can rewire your brain to believe you really can achieve these things, while providing heaps of motivation.

**All that we are is a result of what we have thought.**

BUDDHA

Act on your impulses; they could be a sign from the universe! Try to allow your intuition to guide you. Don't be afraid to step out of your comfort zone.

I am manifesting

the life of my dreams

Certain types of music can be a great way to raise your vibrational frequency. Different sound frequencies are associated with various types of manifestation, allowing you to pick one that aligns with what you are manifesting. YouTube and Spotify are great places to find music with particular sound frequencies. See the next page for popular ones used for manifesting.

Popular sound frequencies for manifesting:

✦ **174 Hz** – relieving pain

✦ **417 Hz** – bringing about change

✦ **528 Hz** – healing of the body

✦ **639 Hz** – healing relationships

✦ **741 Hz** – inspiring creativity

✦ **852 Hz** – harmony within
   yourself and the universe

*Have faith in the magic and miracles of life, for only those that do get to experience them.*

HAL ELROD

One way to maintain a positive mindset is to surround yourself with people that hold similar beliefs and values. Fill your friend circle with like-minded souls and create a network that inspires you to work hard at achieving your dreams. This doesn't mean leaving current friends behind, though!

Have you ever noticed a particular series of three or four repeating digits, like 333 or 8888, that grab your attention? These numbers can be found anywhere – within phone numbers, time stamps or even on digital clocks. In manifesting, these are known as "angel numbers". They are messages from the universe that can offer insight into your journey.

Angel number meanings:

**000** – New opportunities
on the horizon

**111** – You have support
from the universe

**222** – Trust in the process

**333** – Good things are
coming your way

**444** – You are not alone

**555** – Change is coming

**666** – Be kind to yourself

**777** – It's working!

**888** – You are worthy

**999** – Something is
coming to an end

When you visualize, then you materialize. If you've been there in your mind, you'll go there in your body.

DENIS WAITLEY

If you are feeling demoralized at how long it's taking the universe to respond to your manifestations, try reading some of the affirmations that speak to you from this book. Repeat them to yourself daily and be patient. The more you say them, the more you will believe them!

I deserve
everything
I dream,
everything
I dream will
come true

Focus on nourishing your body as well as your mind. Food provides you with energy, so it makes sense to make sure it is good energy! Eating healthily can make you feel good. If you don't feel good, it means you are not in alignment with yourself. The better you feel, the higher your vibrational frequency.

If you respond best to the techniques where you have something physical to work with, try a manifestation box. Find and decorate a box – any size that will fit what you have planned to put in it – and fill it with anything that resonates with your manifestations. Keep coming back to your box for inspiration.

All our dreams
can come true,
if we have
the courage to
pursue them.

**WALT DISNEY**

Don't put it off; act today. Work with the universe. There is always something you can do – it doesn't have to be a grand gesture, so take action now!

There is no reason you can't keep it simple. You don't need to manifest life-altering events. Why not take small steps by manifesting every morning what you want the day to bring? Try scripting in the morning, and then at the end of every day, make a list of your achievements. Celebrate the small wins!

One way to elevate your manifesting could be to create a dedicated, relaxing, manifesting space within your home. Increase the effectiveness of your manifesting by surrounding yourself with visual aids that reflect your end goals. Why not add some candles and crystals, and fairy lights for added ambience?

To accomplish great things we must not only act, but also dream; not only plan, but also believe.

ANATOLE FRANCE

Beware of self-critical thoughts. Low self-esteem can cause reduced feelings of happiness, and therefore lower vibrations. Surround yourself with things that make you happy. Try writing a list of what you are good at and what you like about yourself to give yourself a boost.

If you feel you are getting stuck in a rut, try mixing it up a bit. If the 3-6-9 technique hasn't inspired you, why not switch to the pillow method? If you tend to stick to scripting, give visualization a try. As soon as you begin to feel that manifesting is a chore, try something new.

I attract
good fortune

Make sure you cut out negative language like "can't" or "won't", as these statements can subconsciously affect your overall view of the world. Switch to more positive language to help you feel confident and motivated, enabling you to feel more empowered.

*Whatever the mind can conceive and believe, it can achieve.*

NAPOLEON HILL

When opportunity comes knocking, always open the door! Just because it doesn't look exactly as you imagined, it doesn't mean that it's not good for you. Be open to all possibilities. Surrender your desires to the universe and trust that it will deliver what is best for you. The universe has your back.

Everyday tips when
manifesting your happiness:

+ Do what brings you joy.

+ Show gratitude.

+ Don't focus too much
energy on things that
are not important.

+ Live as if you have
achieved your dreams.

+ Create and read
affirmations daily.

+ Surround yourself
with positivity.

+ Believe you are worthy
of achieving happiness.

Since its rise in popularity, many celebrities have come out endorsing manifesting. Oprah Winfrey, Will Smith, Jim Carrey, Lady Gaga and Arnold Schwarzenegger are just a few of the big names that have claimed they have made positive changes to their lives through manifesting them.

You already have
within you everything
you need to turn your
dreams into reality.

WALLACE D. WATTLES

## THE KEYS TO MANIFESTING SUCCESS #1

✦ You believe that anything is possible.

✦ You surrender your dreams
and desires to the universe.

✦ You are clear and concise
about what you want.

✦ You understand that whatever
energy you put out, you get back.

✦ You believe that the universe has
got your best interests at heart.

The universe
supports me,
I place my trust
in the universe

## THE KEYS TO MANIFESTING SUCCESS #2

✦  You trust in your journey.

✦  You remove doubt.

✦  You are grateful for what you have.

✦  You spend time with people
   who support you.

✦  You commit to making time
   to manifest what you want.

✦  You don't sit back and wait
   for things to come to you.

## TROUBLESHOOTING #1

If things aren't happening, ask yourself these questions:

✦ Are you being clear enough?
  Be as specific as possible!

✦ Are you too focused on what is
  wrong or missing in your life?
  Remember, you need positive
  energy to receive positivity back!

✦ Are you taking action? You
  can't just sit back and wait!

Every single second
is an opportunity to
change your life.

RHONDA BYRNE

## TROUBLESHOOTING #2

+ Are you putting out positive energy?
  Steer clear of toxic situations
  and surround yourself with
  like-minded people.

+ Do you trust the journey?
  If you don't have faith that the
  universe will deliver, it won't!

+ Are you sure you're asking for
  what you really want?
  It's okay to change your mind!

## TROUBLESHOOTING #3

+ Are you reading the signs
  from the universe? Don't let
  opportunities pass you by!

+ Are you too obsessed with
  the outcome? This is a
  common manifestation block.
  Just have some patience
  and enjoy the journey.

+ Are you ensuring you feel
  good? You are worthy of your
  dreams, so don't let self-
  sabotage hold you back!

## GLOSSARY OF TECHNIQUES #1

**3-6-9** – Writing your affirmation three times in the morning, six in the afternoon and nine times in the evening.

**The pillow method** – Place your affirmation under your pillow before going to bed.

**Scripting** – Manifesting through writing.

**Visualization** – Using your imagination to create your future reality.

Feel the power
that comes from
focusing on what
excites you.

OPRAH WINFREY

# GLOSSARY OF TECHNIQUES #2

**55×5** – Write down your affirmation 55 times a day for five days.

**The focus wheel** – Write your dream in a circle and around the outside write any positive thoughts relating to your dream.

**Letter from your future self** – A letter written from the position of having achieved your dreams.

## GLOSSARY OF
## TRICKY TERMS #1

**Affirmation** – A positive statement to help you overcome negative thoughts.

**Alignment** – Being in harmony with your vibrations. You align yourself with your dreams and desires.

**Energy** – Everything is energy, including your thoughts.

**Frequency** – The levels of your vibrations caused by your mindset.

I have the
power to make
my dreams
a reality

## GLOSSARY OF
## TRICKY TERMS #2

**Intentions** – How you are going
to achieve your manifestations.

**Inspired action** – The strong urge to do
something that will help achieve your goal.

**Manifestation blocks** – Obstacles
that inhibit your manifestations.

**Subconscious reprogramming** –
Rewiring your subconscious into believing
you can achieve your dreams.

*It's just about letting the universe know what you want and then working toward it while letting go of how it comes to pass.*

JIM CARREY

## FAREWELL

By harnessing the power of manifestation, you can achieve all the happiness you've ever dreamed of. Just remember, to achieve this you will need: positivity, belief, patience and the willingness to take action. These are the cornerstones to a successful journey. If you can embrace these, you can achieve anything you put your mind to.

Simply by picking up this book, you have made the choice to change your life for the better. However, the path you have chosen isn't always easy: there are going to be times when your beliefs are challenged, and you may find your motivation and patience waning. Don't give up. Reread this book when you need to remind yourself of what you are trying to achieve. If you've worked hard at your manifesting, when your dreams come to fruition, you will feel a great sense of accomplishment. Put your trust in the process – it will be worth it in the end!

Keep looking out for signs and synchronicities that the universe is sending you – you might be seeing these to help you get back on the right track towards happiness. Don't be afraid to step out of your comfort zone if it feels like the right thing to do.

And lastly, enjoy the journey. Good things are coming your way if you just believe!

## MY MANIFESTATION JOURNAL

ISBN: 978-1-80007-829-1

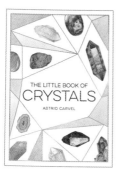

## THE LITTLE BOOK OF CRYSTALS

Astrid Carvel

ISBN: 978-1-78685-959-4

Have you enjoyed this book?
If so, find us on Facebook at
**Summersdale Publishers**,
on Twitter at **@Summersdale** and
on Instagram at **@summersdalebooks**
and get in touch.
We'd love to hear from you!

**www.summersdale.com**

## IMAGE CREDITS